AF507179

Wanda Watercolor

Beth Anne Gold

Copyright © 2022 by beth a gold
All rights reserved.

In her little painted house,
with the painted picket fence,

sits Wanda Watercolor,
in clothes of
colors quite intense.

Its not only the outside of Wanda's house,
that is painted and kept clean.

For once inside you realize,
there's not a dirt spot to be seen.

Everywhere around you,

no matter where one looks,

there lies watercolor paints and
brushes,

and paint by number books.

On the walls of
Wanda's kitchen,

there's a painted
stove and
painted sink.

And when
Wanda feels like
eating,

she paints her
favorite food
and drink.

Upstairs in Wanda's bedroom,
sits a king size
waterbed.
Its one of the most unique I've seen,
it's filled with
watercolors instead!

Now the living
room is the real
masterpiece,

everyone gawks at it
in awe.

For a different detailed
painted scene,
appears on every
wall.

On the east wall is a
pasture,

full of cows and
horses grazing.

While the west wall is a cozy hearth,
inside, a brilliant fire blazing.

The floor, or should I say grass, is

painted different hues of green.

And among its long and
shiny blades,

painted wildflowers can
be seen.

Finally, when looking heavenward,

you'll find the best surprise.

The ceiling and roof have been left off,

revealing the palette of the deep blue skies.

Often heard are "ooh's" and "ah's"
and "wow's" and "golly gee."
"Oh my darling Wanda,
won't you paint my house for me??

How long did it take? and was it hard?"
are questions that most frequently arise.
And at this point, poor Wanda
merely hangs her head and cries.

Now let me explain to all of you
this sad and strange behavior.
After all I'm Wanda's closest friend,
(and also I'm her neighbor.)

You see Wanda is idealistic and impulsive,
sometimes doing things before she thinks.

Like someone who dreams of sailing the oceans,
but only owns a ship that sinks.

Wanda had dreams of her painted home
and the way that is should look.
So her heart did the designing,
ignoring all principles of the book.

Thus when she left the
roof off,

so there'd always be a
view of the skies.

She didn't think far enough ahead
to see that this decision was unwise.

For every time a rainstorm comes,
and the earth is covered in rain.

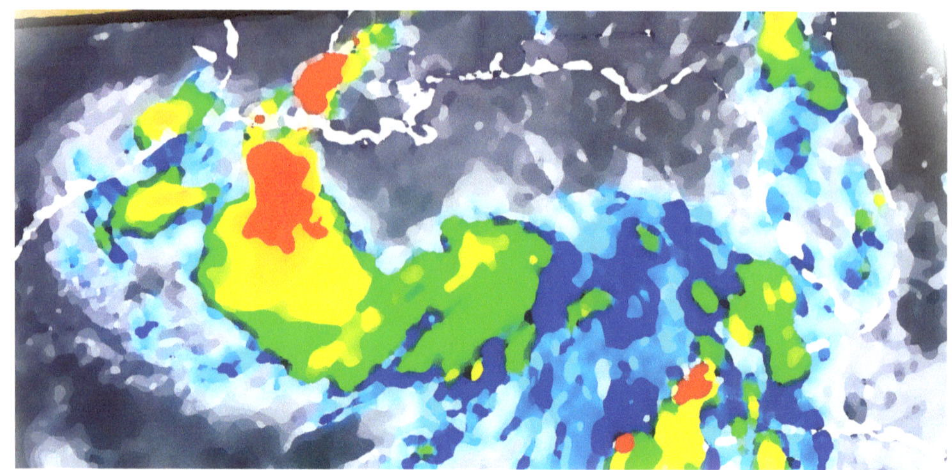

Poor talented, idealistic Wanda
must repaint her world again.

Well I've watched my dear friend Wanda
do this behavior for many years.
Smiling and happy when she's painting,
when it rains, only tears.

I finally said, "dear, Wanda,
why do you always paint the same as you did before?
Flowers growing in the green grass,
that you've painted on the floor?"

"The same curtains on the windows,

the same fireplace on the wall.

The same stovetop in the kitchen,

the same pictures down the hall?"

There was quite a pause of silence,

and then Wanda turned to speak.

There was passion blazing in her eyes,

and a tear upon her cheek.

"I don't mean to keep on painting,
the same images as before.
I mean to paint a brand new doorknob,
so I can open a brand new door.

I mix the colors all so differently

so they'll never be repeated.

I change the layout in my mind,

and how the surfaces are treated.

I decide to change the rooms,

make the kitchen, now the den.

Change décor from Southwest
Native,

to the simple life of Zen.

As you see, my mind's not static,

I'm not purposefully in a rut.

But when my house is a puddle of paint

I'm overwhelmed with a sick feeling in my gut.

When it rains, my mind's a frenzy,

swirling and dripping, like my paint.

The thought of re-creating what I've lost,

makes me sweat and nearly faint.

The project of painting a new life

is first depressing, then exciting.

The sight of my world in a splash of color

is both daunting and inviting.

When I sift through all the feelings

and paint is pooled around my feet.

I recognize another chance

to create self-glory, not self—defeat.

So I pick up my brushes and begin to paint,

on a path I believe is new.

Changing colors, changing rooms,

changing locations and the view.

I think I'm changing everything,

it sure feels different while I do it.

And I don't dare step back to
observe my work,

I wait until I'm finished and I'm
through it.

Amazingly, as I stroll through the
rooms,

I have newly recreated.

It feels homey and familiar,
my sense of purpose re-inflated.

It takes a moment to realize
the familiarity is a curse.

For what I've just finished is
exactly as before.. nothing better,
nothing worse!

Why this keeps on happening,

I've come to finally understand.

As I felt life slipping through my fingers,

like the ocean through the sand.

I've learned
that there
are pictures,

embedded
in the
recesses of
my mind.

And if I
keep my
mind
closed,

the same
old pictures
make me
blind.

Blind to creating new scenes,

with only old, imprinted pictures in my view.

So when I pick up my brushes to paint,

I sadly end up the same as I always do.

So I'm going to change the way I'm living,

I don't want to continue my life with dread.

Knowing my walls will be dripping from all the rain,

and despairing, because I know what lies ahead.

I'm going back to basics,

to rethink my house design.

I'm sure a roof is what is needed,

so I'll make it one of a kind.

It will be a giant skylight,

made entirely of glass.

The view of the heavens still wide open,

and my creations will finally last."

Jubilant with her idea,

Wanda finished the roof in no time flat.

Smiling skyward with fulfillment,

on her painted sofa, she happily sat.

The heavens opened and the rains did come,

and Wanda's house was gleefully dry.

Warm and cozy, she admired her paintings.

Relieved, she gave a joyful cry.

But after several months of relaxing,

Wanda felt her life was a bore.

After the rains, no puddles of paint,

no interior destruction to restore.

"Well this won't do either," Wanda said to herself,

the realization making her quite dizzy.

I see that my constantly ruined interiors,

were actually keeping me happily busy.

With no new scenes for her to paint,

and staring from floor to roof to wall.

Wanda, overcome with regret,

reached out and gave me, her neighbor a call.

She told me in a teary voice,

that without the threat of rain,

She didn't need to keep repainting her home

and the lack of creativity was causing her pain.

I told Wanda I'd be right over,

so that we could devise a plan.

That would satisfy her need to paint,

and I vowed to help her all I can.

I suggested that we bring together

all of our acquaintances and friends.

And create a series of painting parties,

so the painting never ends.

I said "Weekly, monthly, or once per year,

Wanda, you can decide yourself.

When to whitewash your walls and start again,

and pull your paints and brushes off the shelf.

The weather outside won't control your life,

you will create when you are ready.

You can finally enjoy your painting life,

not highs and lows, just keep it steady."

Wanda was overcome with peace,

imagining her house as a canvas
white and new.

Dreams of community painting and
joint creations,

and perhaps she could give a
lesson or two.

"That's it, she cried, tears of
joy in her eyes,

the best idea I've ever
heard.

When I dreamt of my house,
it was only for me,

and now I see how I have
erred.

We need each other, we just think we don't,

so we go on creating our lives in a bubble.

And we only reach out from ourselves to another

when we are lonely or in trouble.

But the need to create is universal,

and the world is made better by collaboration.

So by inviting others to share in the joy,

my painting will be a wellspring of cooperation."

Wanda turned to me with sheer gratitude,

at first not finding her voice.

Then grabbing my hands, she twirled me around,

and she said as we began to rejoice.

"Through the many years in my painted house,

you've helped me learn to make my life as I please.

Only by thinking of new ways to end my struggles

can I now envision a life of ease.

I don't know what I'd do without you,

you've been with me on my darkest days.

I feel so grateful for you, my friend,

reminding me there's sunshine behind the haze. "

And that is the story of my friend Wanda,

who became known as the watercolor queen.

She contentedly lived in her unique little house,

an ever-changing, evolving scene.

www.ingramcontent.com/pod-product-compliance
Lightning Source LLC
Chambersburg PA
CBHW040931110726

48006CB00001B/145

9798367088267